Inscriptions
from the
Old Cemetery
in
Rowley, Massachusetts

George B. Blodgette, Esq

HERITAGE BOOKS
2008

HERITAGE BOOKS

AN IMPRINT OF HERITAGE BOOKS, INC.

Books, CDs, and more—Worldwide

For our listing of thousands of titles see our website
at
www.HeritageBooks.com

Published 2008 by
HERITAGE BOOKS, INC.
Publishing Division
100 Railroad Ave. #104
Westminster, Maryland 21157

International Standard Book Numbers
Paperbound: 978-0-7884-4899-7
Clothbound: 978-0-7884-7608-2

APPENDIX.

The following list includes all the inscriptions now (1892) to be found in that part of the cemetery in use before 1830.

Two gravestones were last year moved to the addition of 1830.

This cemetery was the only one used by the town of Rowley to 1702, when the burial ground in Byfield Parish was first used. The first burial in the Second Parish of Rowley, now George-town, was in 1732. There is a cemetery in Rowley, within the limits of the Linebrook Parish, used as early as 1747; it is now without inscriptions, is wholly abandoned, and its site known to but few.

The words and figures in brackets above each inscription indicate where the same may be found in the rows of stones on the east and west side of Central Avenue, entering from Main street.

Thus [6 Row West 3] indicates the sixth row from the gate on the west side of Central Avenue and the third stone from the Avenue in that row.

[No. 1, 6 Row, West 3.]

Mr JAMES BAILY
DIED MARCH Ye 20th
1714 × 15 AGED
64 YEARS

AS YOU ARE
SOE WEARE WE
BUT AS WE ARE
YOU SHALL BE

[No. 2, 4 Row, West 2.]

HERE LIES Ye
BODY OF Mr
NATHANIEL
BAYLEY WHO
DIED JULY Ye
21st 1722 IN
THE 48th
YEAR OF
HIS AGE

[No 3, 17 Row, West 3.]

HERE LIES Ye
BODY OF MRS
SARAH BAYLEY
Ye WIFE OF CAPT
JONATHAN BAYLEY
WHO DIED SEPTEMR
Ye 28 1730   IN
Ye 55th YEAR OF
HER AGE

[No. 4, 4 Row, East 4. (Brick.)]

In Memory of
Dean David Baily
who died May 12th
1769 *in 62 year of his age*

[No. 5, 21 Row, West 3.]

In memory of
SARAH BAILEY,
who died
April 28 1799
Æt 52

Farewell dear friends I shall lie here
Till time shall end, and Christ appear.

[No. 6, 7 Row, East 2.]

DOCTER DAUID
BENNET WHO DIED
FEBRUARY Ye 4 1718/9
AGED 103 YEARS.

[No. 7, 6 Row, West 2.]

HERE LIES THE
BODY OF DOC^T
WILLIAM BENNET
WHO DIED
SEPTEMBER Y^e
18th 1724 IN
Y^e 38th YEAR
OF HIS AGE

[No. 8, 6 Row, West 7.]

JOHN BOYNTON
SON OF JOHN
& BETHIAH
DIED : OCTOBER
Y^e 19 1714
AGED 5
MONTHS

[No. 9, 13 Row, West 3.]

HERE LYES Y^e
BODY OF JOSEPh
SON OF HILKIAH
& PRISCILLA
BOYNTON WHO
DIED FEBRUARY
Y^e 7 1717–18
AGED 2 MONTHS
& 3 DAYS

[No. 10, 14 Row, West 4.]

HERE LYES Y^e BODY
OF Mr JOHN BOY-
ENTON WHO DIED
OCTOBER Y^e 8 1718
& IN Y^e 40th YEARE
OF HIS AGE

[No. 11, 17 Row, West 4.]

HERE LIES Y^e BODY
OF CAP^T JOSEPH
BOYNTON WHO DIED
DECEMBER 16, 1730
AGED ABOUT 85 YEARS

MAKE CHRIST YOUR FRIEND
BEFORE YOU DIE THAT
YOU MAY LIVE ETERNAL

[No. 12, 5 Row, East 1.]

Memento mori

In
Memory of
Mrs DOROTHY BRADFORD

8

consort of Rev. *Moses Bradford*
of *Frances-Town* (*N. H.*)
*who died June y*e 24*th*
AD 1792 *Ætat.* 26 —

Farewell Dear friend a short farewell
Till we again shall meet above
In the sweet groves where pleasures dwell
And trees of life bear fruits of love.
Time how short!! Eternity how long!!!
Blessed are the Dead that die in the Lord.

[No. 13, 5 Row, East 4 (The oldest stone)].

HEAR LYS WHAT WAS
MORTAL OF Yᵉ WORTHY
CAP MOSES BRADStREEt
DESEASED AUGUST Yᵉ
17ᵗʰ 1690 & IN Yᵉ 47ᵗʰ
YEAR OF HIS AGE
FRIENDS & RELATIONS
YOU MIGHT BEHOLD
A LAMB OF GOD
FItt FOR Yᵉ FOLD

[No. 14, 5 Row, East 5.]

HERE LYES Yᵉ
BODY OF BREGET
DAUGHTER OF Mʳ
MOSES & Mʳˢ HAN-
NAH BRADSTREET
DIED JULY Yᵉ 22
1718 AGED 22
YEARS & 4
MONTHS

[No. 15, 5 Row, East 6.]

HERE LIES Yᵉ BODY
OF JOHN
BRADSTREET Yᵉ
SON OF Mᴿ MOSES
AND MRˢ HANNAH
BRADSTREET WHO
DIED MAY Yᵉ 24
1724 AGED 24
YEARS

[No. 16, 5 Row, East 7.]

HERE LIES THE
BODY OF MR
MOSES BRODSTRET
JUN^R WHO DIED
FEBRUARY 15 1727
AGED 29 YEAR^s

[No. 17, 16 Row, East 10.]

HERE LIES THE·
BODY OF MR^s
HANNAH BRADSTREET
THE WIFE OF MR
MOSES BRADSTREET WHO
DIED JANUARY THE 3
1737 AGED 67 YEARS

[No. 18, 16 Row, East 9.]

HERE LIES THE
BODY OF MR
MOSES BRADSTREET
WHO DECEASED
DECEMBER THE
20 1737 IN
THE 73 YEAR
OF HIS AGE.

[No. 19, 16 Row, East 11.]

HERE LIES Y^e BODY
OF MR^s HANNAH
BRADSTREET THE
WIFE OF MR NATHANIEL
BRADSTREET WHO
DEC^T APRIL Y^e 11
1739 AGED 36 YEARS
& 2 MONTHS

[No. 20, 10 Row, East 3.]

Here Lies The Body
of Mrs Dorothy
Bradstret Late Rel^{it} to
Mr Moses Bradstret Form^{ly}
Widdo & Rel^{it} to Capt
Ezekiel Northend Who
Died June the 17 AD
1752 Aged 84 Years

[No. 21, 16 Row, East 12.]

HERE LIES
THE BODY OF
LEU^T NATHANIE^L
BRADSTREET WHO
DIED DECEMBER
THE 2 1752
IN THE 48 YEAR
OF HIS AGE

[No. 22, 16 Row, East 13.]

HERE LIES BURIED
THE BODY OF M^{rs}
ABIGAIL THE WIFE
OF Mr EZEKIEL
BRADSTREET WHO
DIED AUGUS^T THE
23^D 1773 IN
THE 22 YEAR
OF HER AGE

[No 23, 16 Row, West 9.]

In memory of
THOMAS
Son of Moses &
Sarah Bradstreet
who died June 27 1800
in the 6 year of his age

Happy infant early blest,
Rest, in peaceful slumbers rest,
Early rescu'd from the cares
Which increase with growing years.

[No. 24, 18 Row, West 7.]

In memory of
Nathaniel Bradstreet
who died March 28 1806
Aged 66 Years

Though cold the sod dear friend, that weeps thy clay,
Thus lowly once the world's great Saviour lay,
Sweet be thy slumbers and thy rest serene
Till the last trump shall wake the glorious scene
Till He whose voice bade Lazarus arise
Shall rouse his slumbering saints, and call them to the skies.

[No. 25, 5 Row, East 3.]

Lieut
MOSES BRADSTREET
died Nov. 1. 1811.
Æt. 83.

He was a kind husband, an indulgent
parent, and useful citizan.

He was a patriot & a christian
He resigned his temporal interest
in the hope of an Eternal Crown

Come, children go with us to glory

[No. 26, 16 Row, West 8.]

Thomas
son of Mr. Moses &
Mrs Mary Bradstreet
died July 10. 1813.
Æt. 3.

Ah! Death couldst thou
not spare his youthful bloom
But summon'd him so early
to the tomb

[No. 27, 18 Row, West 6.]

In memory of
Phebe,
widow of
Nathaniel Bradstreet,
who died Dec. 18, 1815.
Aged 74 years.

A soul prepared needs no delays,
The summons come the saint obeys;
Swift was the flight and short the road,
She clos'd her eyes and saw her God.

[No. 28, 5 Row, East 2.]

Mrs.
Lucy Bradstreet
Relict of
Lieu^t Moses Bradstreet,
died June 9 1816
Æt. 88.

She filled the various relations of a
daughter wife, mother, with propriety
affection, and usefulness.

She was a decided friend to morality
piety and evangelical religion
Christ was her hope, her joy, her life.

[No. 29, 10 Row, West 8.]

Mrs
ELIZABETH
wife of
Mr Nath¹ Bradstreet,
died July 11. 1827.
Æt. 51.
Blessed are the dead who die in the
Lord

[No. 30, 16 Row, West 11 (Marble).]

MOSES BRADSTREET
DIED
Oct. 23, 1829,
Aged 76.

[No. 31, 16 Row, West 12 (Marble).]

SARAH
wife of
Moses Bradstreet
DIED
Sept. 8, 1851
Aged 97

[No. 32, 13 Row, West 6.]

HERE LIES MARY
BURPE Yᵉ WIFE
OF THOMAS
BURPE DIED Yᵉ
17ᵗʰ DAY OF
AUGUST 1721
IN Yᵉ 24ᵗʰ
YEAR OF HER
AGE

[No. 33, 15 Row, West 3.]

HERE LIES
ESTHEᴙ BURPE
Yᵉ WIFE OF
THOMAS BURPE
SENER DIED
OCTOBER Yᵉ
30 1722 IN
THE 55
YEAR OF HER
AGE

[No. 34, 15 Row, West 1.]

HERE LIES Y^e
BODY OF
JEREMIAH
BURPE WHO
DIED FEBRUAR^y
Y^e 4th 1723
IN THE 32nd
YEAR OF
HIS AGE

[No. 35, 13 Row, West 2.]

HERE LIES Y^e BODY
OF DAUID BURPE
WHO DIED DECEMB^R
Y^e 13 1728 IN
THE 28 YEAR
OF HIS AGE

[No. 36, 12 Row, West 2.]

HERE LIES Y^e BODy
OF NATHAN
BURPE WHO DIED
JANUARY Y^e 22
1729 IN Y^e 25
YEAR OF HIS
AGE

[No. 37, 12 Row. West 1.]

HERE LIES Y^e BODY
OF HANNAH BURPE
Y^e WIFE OF JONATH^N
BURPE WHO DIED
IANUARY Y^e 24th
1729 IN Y^e
24th YEAR OF
HER AGE

[No. 38, 21 Row, West 1.]

HERE LIES
THE BODY OF
MR^s JOHANNAH
BURPY Y^e WIFE
OF MR JOSEPH
BURPY WHO
DIED OCTOBER
THE 1 1748 IN
THE 28 YEAR
OF HER AGE

[No. 39, 1 Row, East 8].

THIS IN MEMORY OF
MR JOSEPH BURPEY
WHO DIED JANUARY
THE 5th 1776 AND
IN THE 57th YEAR
OF HIS AGE

My flesh shall slumber in the
Ground Till the last trumpets
Joyful sound Then bursts the
Chains with sweet surprise, And
in my Saviours image rise

[No. 40, 6 Row, West 1.]

SAMEUL CALIF

DIED

April 26, 1845,
Æt. 35.

[No. 41, 10 Row, West 5]
Here lies the body of
Deac. JOSEPH CHAPLIN,
food for worms till the glorious
resurrection morning.   He was born Feb. 22
1752 & died Dec. 12, 1813.
Deceitful world farewell to you,
In heaven may I appear,
I bid you friends a short adieu
And will you meet me there;
And join the saints with angels bright
To praise the Sacred Three,
And dwell with him in realms of light
Who dy'd to make us free.
Then while the grave's before your eyes
Pray give this truth its weight
That on a moment as it flies
Hangs your eternal state.
Haste thou my soul arise and fly
Thro' realms of lasting day
And say there's nought below the sky
To tempt thee there to stay
Here my redeemer reigns with praise
And always from his throne,
·He watches all my dust to raise
A body like his own.

[No. 42, 10 Row, West 6.]

RUTH CHAPLIN

Died

Jan. 28 1843;

Aged 90 y$\underline{^m}$ &

Six days

[No. 44, 10 Row, West 1.]

HERE LYES BURIED Y^e
BODY OF Mr EBENEZE$_R$
CLARK WHO DIED
APRIL Y^e 28 1716
IN Y^e 29 YEAR OF
HIS AGE

AS YOU ARE SO WERE
WE BUT AS WE ARE SO
YOU WILL BE

[No. 43, 10 Row, West 2.]

IOHN CHOATE
SON OF M^r ROB^T
& M^{r}S EUNICE
CHOATE DIED
OCTOBR Y^e 27
1718 AGED 4
MONTHS &
28 DAYS

[No. 45, 12 Row, East 6.]

HERE LIES Y^e
BODEY OF ARON
CLARK SON TO MR
JONAT^{h}AN CLARK
WHO DIED MARCH
Y^e 10 1743 IN Y^e
21 YEAR OF
HIS AGE

[No. 46, 15 Row, East 9 (Marble)].

Here lies buried
the body of
M$_{RS}$ SARAH NORTHEN,
consort of
Dr. Nathaniel Cogswell,
who departed this life
March 8, 1773,
in the 35 year of her age
and their
still born infant
Also
their son
WADE COGSWELL E$_{SQR.}$
who died
16, Feb. 1855,
aged 86 years.

9

[No. 47, 1 Row, West 12.]

MISS DOROTHY,
daughter of
Doct. Nathaniel &
Mrs Lois Cogswell,
Obit. Feb. 15. 1805.
Æt. 24.

[No. 48, 15 Row, East 8.]

Sacred
To the memory of
DOCTOR NATH^L COGSWELL
who died 25. of May, 1822
Aged 83 years

Erect of figure, as his soul upright,
And eye benignant, as his breast serene
His course was blameless and beneficent
The vision sure was pleasant but is past.

[No. 49, 15 Row, East 7.]

Sacred
to the memory of
MRS LOIS,
Relict of the late
Dr. Nathl Cogswell,
who died Aug : 21 1825
Æt. 83.

Blessed are the dead which die in the
Lord hence forth yea saith the spirit
that they may rest from their
labors & their works do
follow them

[No. 50, 12 Row, West 6.]

In memory of
Miss Mary Cooper,
who died

Nov. 12, 1815,
Æt. 76.

Here in the silent grave I lie,
No more the scenes of life to try,
And you dear friends, I leave behind
Must soon this gloomy mansion find.

[No. 51, 9 Row, West 2.]

TAMAR CRES-
SEY (DAUGHTER
OF MICHAEL
& SARAH CRES
SEY) DIED MAY
Y^e 29 1716
AGED NEERE
19 YEARS.

[No. 52, 12 Row, West 4.]

HERE LYES Y^e
BODY OF WILLIAM
CRESEY WHO
DIED FEBRUARY
Y^e 9th 1717–18
AGED 55 YEARS

[No. 53, 9 Row, West 3.]

HERE LIES
MIKAEL CRECI$_{IUN}^{R}$
DIED JULY
15th 1720
AGED 32
YEARS

[No. 54, 12 Row, West 8.]

The House appointed for all living.

Lieut.
MARK CREASEY
died
May 4. 1816.
Æt. 82.

The tyrant death, 'tho held in long delay,
Is sure at last to sieze his destin'd prey ;
But death disarm'd, no victory shall achieve ;
For they are sure to conquor, that believe.

[No. 55, 2 Row, East 14.]

HERE LIES ye BODYS OF
JACOB MARY & MOSES DAUI^s
ye CHILDREN OF MR MOSES &
MR^s HANNAH DAUIS JACOB
DIED FEB 26th 1729 IN
ye 16th YEAR OF HIS AGE
MARY DIED FEB 27th 1729
& IN ye 6 YEAR OF
HER AGE MOSES DIED
MAR 3 1729 IN ye 4 YEAR
OF HIS AGE

[No. 56, 16 Row, East 6.]

HERE LIES
THE BODY OF
CAP^T MOSES
DAUIS WHO
DIED FEBRUAry
Y^e 1   1753 IN
The 63 YEAR
OF HIS AGE

[No. 57, 9 Row, West 1.]

HERE LYES
Y^e BODY OF
JAMES DICKINSO^N
AGED ABOUT 27
YEARS DESEEASE^D
IANVARY Y^e 5th
1 7 0 5

[No. 58, 8 Row, West 3 (Marble).]

MR PHINEAS DODGE
Died March 4, 1824.
Aged 78 years.

"The memory of the
just is blessed."

[No. 59, 8 Row, West 4 (Marble).]

In Memory of
LUCY DODGE
Relict of
PHINEAS DODGE,
who died
March 30 AD. 1837;
in the 92 year
of her age.

[No. 60, 1 Row, West 13.]

Mr
LEVI DOLE
died
March 7. 1830
Æt. 47.

[No. 61, 16 Row, West 6.]

HERE LIES Y^e BODY
OF ELISABETH DRESSER
DAUGHTER OF MR
JOSEPH & MR^s JOANNA
DRESSER WHO DIED
MAY Y^e 30 1736 AGED
19 YEARS 5 MONTHS
& 25 DAYS

HERE LET REMAIN
HER UNDESTURBED
DUST UNTILL THE
RESURRECTION OF
THE JUST

[No. 62, 14 Row, East 3.]

HERE LIES THE
BODY OF DOC^T
AMOS DRESSER
WHO DIED
SEPTEMBER Y^e 22
A D 1741 IN
Y^e 29 YEAR
OF HIS AGE

[No. 63, 14 Row, West 6 (Marble.)]

Mr
David Edgerly
was drowned in
Rowley River, Mass.
August 11 1816
in the 25 year
of his age

Intered in Rowley

[No. 64, 14 Row, East 7.]

HERE LIES
Y^e BODEY OF
MR^s MARY
ELLSWORTH Y^e WIFE
OF JEREMIAH ELLS
WORTH JUN^R WHO
DIED DECEMBER
Y^e 10 1742 IN Y^e
25 YEAR OF
HER AGE

[No. 65, 14 Row, East 1.]

HERE LIES Y^e
BODY OF MR
NATHAN FRAZER
WHO DIED OCTOBER
THE 21 1741
IN Y^e 42
YEAR OF HIS
AGE

[No. 66, 2 Row, West 4.]

HERE LYES
Y^e BODY OF
SARAH GAGE
Y^e DAUGHTER
OF WILLIAM
& MERCY
GAGE WHO
DIED JUNE
18 1713
AGED 5 YEARS

[No. 67, 16 Row, West 4.]

HERE LIES Yᵉ BODY
OF MR WILLIAM GAGE
WHO DIED MARCH
Yᵉ 18ᵗʰ 1730
IN Yᵉ 48
YEAR OF HIS
AGE

[No. 68, 16 Row, West 5.]

In Memory of
Mʳˢ MERCY GAGE
widow of
Mʳ WILLIAM GAGE
who died [Oct. 10 1775]
In her 93ᵈ year

In Adam all Die, in Christ
shall all be made alive

[No. 69, 1 Rqw, East 4 (Marble).]

WILLIAM GAGE
eldest son of
Col. Thomas Gage
DIED
Oct. 2, 1777
Æt. 26 y'rs

He was a dutiful child, an obliging ✦
Husband, and a tender Parent,
He lived beloved and died lamented

[No. 70, 6 Row, East 1].

Memento Mori

Here lies
Interred the body of
Col THOMAS GAAGE
who Departed this Life
August the 31ˢᵗ AD 1788
Aged 77 years & 19 days

The old, the wise, the rich, and great,
Must prostrate lie, in humble state,
There's none that's free from death's alarms
We all must lie, in his cold arms—
Let Mourning friends & kindred dear
Lament the dead, Repent and fear
Let Youth & Children read this stone
Feel they must die, & soon be gone

[No. 71, 2 Row, West 7.]

To the Memory
of MRS MARY GAGE,
Consort of Mr THO^S GAGE,
who departed this life June
26th 1798, aged 34 years, 9
Months & 11 days

Ah hapless Mother! scarce had thy fond arms
Clasp'd the sweet Babe to thy maternal breast
Ere death's sad harbinger spread wide alarms,
And drove the smiling cherub from its rest.

The tender partner of thy joys & cares ;
The smiling pledge which heaven in mercy
(gave ;
The aged Father, pious Mothers prayers—
Could not avail to save the from
(the grave.

[No. 72, 18 Row, West 4.]

Mrs Jane Gage
Consort of
Mr Nathaniel Gage
died April 30th 1801
Ætat. 77

Beneath this stone death's prisoner lies,
The stone shall move the prisoner rise
When Jesus with Almighty word
Calls his dead saints to meet their Lord.

[No. 73, 6 Row, East 2.]

In Memory of
MRS APPHIA GAGE
Relict of
Col. Thomas Gage
who died Augst 26, 1804
Æt. 88

Here let remain her undisturbed dust
Untill the resurection of the just

[No. 74, 18 Row, West 3.]

Sacred to the
Memory of
Mᵣ NATHANIEL GAGE,
who departed this life
Oct. 21ˢᵗ 1807,
Aged 81 years.

Through varied scenes past three score years & ten
I liv'd on earth, & dwelt with mortal men:
Twas but a point.   Eternity how vast.
Where scenes forever new, forever last

(This stone was erected by his daughter)
Jane Gage

[No. 75, 2 Row, West 5.]	[No. 76, 2 Row, West 6.]
Miss	Miss
EDNAH GAGE,	MARY GAGE
Daughtᵣ of Maj. Thomas	Daughtᵣ of Maj. Thomas
& Mrs Mary Gage	& Mrs Mary Gage
died Jan. 5, 1811,	died Nov. 8. 1812
Æt. 23.	Æt. 28.

[No. 77, 2 Row, West 8 (Marble).]

MAJOR THOMAS GAGE,
born Feb. 21, 1755 ; died Aug. 10, 1816.
Mary, his wife, born Sept. 15, 1763, died June 27, 1798
Their children, Viz.

William,	born May	5, 1783, died Oct. 13, 1820.
Mary,	" Jan.	29, 1785, " Nov. 8, 1812.
Apphia,	" Jan.	5, 1787, " Nov. 14, 1818.
Ednah,	" May	23, 1789, " Jan. 5, 1811.
Thomas,	" March	1, 1791, " Feb. 12, 1822.
Moses,	" March	29, 1793, " Feb. 24, 1827,
	In Havana.	
Elizabeth,	" Aug.	31, 1795, " Jan. 1, 1830,

In Ipswich.

Daniel,   " Feb. 11, 1798, died Oct. 5, 1798,
Lucy, a 2^d wife, born May 5, 1760,
died July 27, 1809.

The pale consumption gave the dreadful blow,
The event was fatal; 'tho the effects were slow.

[No. 78, 2 Row, West 11 (Marble).]

WILLIAM GAGE

DIED

Oct. 13, 1820.

Æt. 38 ys. 5 ms.

———— : ————

LUCY

His wife

DIED

Mar. 15, 1870,

Æt. 86 ys. 8 ds.

———— : ————

Also their children died
WILLIAM June 9, 1817. Æt. 1 yr. 9 ms.
MARY E. Feb. 18, 1819. Æt. 1 yr. 4 ms.
LUCY M. June 10, 1820. Æt. 4 ms.

[No. 79, 2 Row, West 10.]

In memory of
THOMAS GAGE J$_R$
who died
Feb. 12, 1822,
aged 31.

[No. 80, 13 Row, East 2.]

Here Lie Y^e Remains of
MI^{ss} MEHETABEL GIBSON
Consort of Dc^n Benjn
Gibson & Dc^n humphr^y
Hobson Who Departed
this Life MAY Y^e 14 1773
Æt 84   She Livd to
A good old age in
preparation For & Died
In hope of the
Heavenly Inheritance

10

[No. 81, 16 Row, West 2.]

HERE LIES Y^e BODY
OF Y^e HONOURABEL
THOMAS HALE ESQ^R
WHO DIED APRIL
Y^e 11th 1730
IN Y^e 72
YEAR OF HIS
AGE

[No. 82, 16 Row, West 3.]

HERE LIES
Y^e BODY OF MR^s
SARAH HALE Y^e
UERTUOVS WIFE
ESQ^R
OF THOMAS HALE
WHO DIED APRIE^L
Y^e 26 1732
AGED 70 YEARS

[No. 84, 1 Row, West 2.]

Erected to the memo-
ry of Mrs Jane Hale,
widow of the late
Dr. William Hale, who
departed this life
July 5 1799 in the 57
year of her age

[No. 83, 1 Row, West 1.]

In Memory
of
DOCT^R WILLIAM HALE
who died
Febr^y 21st 1784,
in the 56 year
of his age

[No. 86, 16 Row, West 10 (Marble).]

Mrs
IRENE
wife of
Mr Daniel Hale, J^r
died Aug. 31 1823.
Æt 30

[No. 85, 2 Row, West 12 (Marble).]

In Memory of
Mr. MOSES HALE,
of Salem, who died
Oct. 1, 1822
Aged 49.

A kind and affectionate wife
an obedient daughter
the much lov'd sister
the obliging friend

But the fair youth is gone
The much lov'd object fled
Enter'd her long eternal home
And number'd with the dead

[No. 87, 3 Row, West 4.]

Mr
DANIEL HALE
died
Jan. 31, 1827.
Æt. 76.

A tendar Husband, Father dear,
A sincere Friend, lies buried here,
Virtue in him a friend could find,
To him 'twas pleasing to be kind.

[No. 88, 3 Row, West 5 (Marble).]

ELIZABETH
relict of
DANIEL HALE
died
Nov. 11, 1833;
Aged 77.

———

Erected by her daughter.

[No. 89, 3 Row, East 2.]

HERE LYETH BURIED
Yᵉ BODY OF MIS· SARAH
HAMMOND (WIFE OF
Mʳ THOMAS HAM-
MOND) WHO DIED
JANUARY Yᵉ 16 1712/13
AGED 57 YEARS

[No. 90, 3 Row, East 1.]

1740
HERE LIES Yᵉ BODY OF MR
THOMAS HAMMOND DECSᵀ
FEBUARY Yᵉ 26ᵗʰ 1724
IN THE 69ᵗʰ YEAR
OF HIS AGE.

[No. 91, 23 Row, West 1.]

Here Lies the
Body of Mr Oliver
Hammand Who
Died Septʳ the
19 A. D. 1758
in the 29 Year
of his Age

[No. 92, 9 Row, East 1.]

HERE LIES Yᵉ BODY
OF DEACON TIMOTHʸ
HARRIS WHO DIED
MARCH Yᵉ 24ᵗʰ 1723
IN Yᵉ 66ᵗʰ YEAR
OF HIS AGE

[No. 93, 1 Row, East 12.]

In Memory of
Mrs EUNICE HARRIS
wife of Mr JOHN HARRIS
who died Sept ye 21st A. D.
1775 In ye 39th year of her
Age   How lov.d
how valu.d, once avail thee not
To whom Related or by whom begot,
A Heap of Dust alone Remains of thee :
Tis all thou art;
And all the Proud Shall be.

[No. 94, 1 Row, West 7.]

In Memory of
Miss Mary Harris eldest
daughter of Mr John &
Mrs Eunice Harris
who made her exit from
this mutable world Nov^r
11th 1795 aged 28 years &
5 months

[No. 95, 1 Row, West 8.]

Here lies the body of
LIEU. JOHN HARRIS
who departed this life
Oct. 7. 1805 in the 34
year of his Age

A kind husband a loving parent
A dutiful son an honest and
An upright citizen much respected
In his life & equally regretted
in his death
Stop kind traveller, pause & view
The hollow tomb prepar'd for you

[No. 96, 1 Row, West 6 (Marble).]

Sacred to the Memory
of
JOHN HARRIS
who died
Sept. 20 1808
in his 78th year

[No. 97, 1 Row, West 9.]

Mr.
TIMOTHY HARRIS
Died March 11. 1818
Æt. 81.

A pious Christian, and a friend sincere,
A tender husband, to his children dear,
Virtue in him a friend could find,
In him twas pleasing to be kind.

———

He's gone alas! nor could he stay,
To dwell with mortals here in clay
His spirit still we hope doth sing
The praise of God the heavenly King

[No. 98, 1 Row, West 10.]

Mrs
EUNICE,
relict of
Mr Timothy Harris
died Aug : 27. 1829.
Æt 90.

Mortals, how few among our race
Have given this thought its weight,
That on the present moment hangs,
Your everlasting fate.

[No. 99, 15 Row, West 4.]

HERE LIES
THOMAS HART
SON OF JOSEPH
HART & JANE
HART DIED
OCTOBER Y^e 23
1722 IN Y^e
17 YEAR OF
HIS AGE

[No. 100, 12 Row, West 3.]

M^{r}S
MARY
HARTSHORN

(Foot stone in place of headstone, broken and lost.)

[No. 101, 2 Row, East 1.]

In Memory of
Mrs Sarah
Haseltine who
Died Au^t The 13^h
1778 in the
56^h year
of her age

[No. 102, 2 Row, East 12.]

HERE LIES Y^e BODY
OF MR WILLIAM
HOBSON WHO
DIED SEPTEMBER
ye 23 1725 IN
ye 67th YEAR OF
HIS AGE

[No. 103, 13 Row, West 9.]

HERE LIES Y^e
BODY OF WILLIAM
HOBSON^{JUNER} WHO
DIED JUNE Y^e 2
1727 IN Y^e 27
YEAR OF HIS
AGE

[No. 104, 14 Row, East 2.]

HERE LIES THE
BODY OF MR JEREMIAH
HOBSON WHO DIED
SEPTEMBER THE 13
1741 BEING 44
YEARS & 3 DAYS

[No. 105, 13 Row, East 1.]

HERE LIES Y^e
BODY OF DECK^n
HUMPHRY HOBSON
WHO DIED JUN
THE 23^d A D
1742 AGED 57
YEARS A 11 MON^t
AND 13 DAYS

[No. 106, 22 Row, West 2.]

HERE LIES the BODY
of
Mrs Hannah Hobson
the wife of Mr
William Hobson
Who Died Sept^r
the 13th 1757 in
the 28th year
of her age

[No. 107, 13 Row, East 3.]

Here Lie Interred
the Remains of ye hon^{ble}
HUMPHRY HOBSON ESQ^r
Who Died In the Midst
of his Growing
Usefulnes^s & honor
Au^g ye 2^d 1773 Æt 56
He Was an Ornament
to his Town & Father
to his Country proh Dolo^y

[No. 109, 13 Row, East 5.]

Here Lie the Earthly
Remains of Miss
MEHETABEL HOBSON
Who Left this Life as
We trust For a better
SEP^t Y^e 9 1773 Æt 27
She Was the Eldest
Amiable & Virtuous
Daut^r of the hon^{ble}
Humphry and
priscilla hobson

[No 111, 10 Row, West 4.]

HEAR LIES MR^s
ELISEBATH
HOPKINSON
WIFE OF MR
JONATHAN
HOPKINSON
DIED MARCH
Y^e 9th 1718
AGED 68
YEAR^s

[No. 108,13 Row, East 4].

Under this Earth Is
Buried the Mortal
part of Miss ELISABETH
HOBSON Who Died
AU^g Y^e 23 1773 Æt 25
the 2^d Daut^r of the
Honble Humphry
Hobson ESQ^r And
Priscilla His Wife
She Left this Shore
In Full Ashurance
of Everlasting Life

[No. 110, 5 Row, West 2.]

ERECTED
In Memory of
Mrs JANE HOLT,
wife of
Mr Joseph Holt,
who died
April 8. 1818.
aged 37 years.

[No. 112, 14 Row, West 2.]

HERE LIES MR son
JONATHAN HOPKIN
DIED FEBRUARY
Y^e 11th 1719
AGED 76 YEARS

[No. 113, 1 Row, East 10.]

In Memory of
Mrs SUSANNA HOSKINS
From Boston Ob^t June
27th 1775
Aged 71 years

[No. 114, 6 Row, West 5.]

HERE LYS Y^e BODY OF
IEREMIAH IEWET
WHO DIED MAY
Y^e 20 1714
AGED 77

[No. 115, 6 Row, West 6.]

MOSES JUET
(SON OF JERE
MIAH & ELIZABETH
JEWET) DIED
IUNE Y^e 11th 1715
IN Y^e 20th YEAR
OF HIS AGE

[No. 116, 8 Row, East 2.]

HERE LYES Y^e BO-
DY OF Mrs FAITH
JEWET, WIFE TO
DECON EZEKIEL
JEWET DIED
OCTO^r Y^e 15 1715 &
IN Y^e 74 YEARE
OF HER AGE

[No. 117, 13 Row, West 8]
(broken.)

HERE LYES Y^e
BODY OF M^r BEN
IAMIN JEWET
WHO DIED
JANUARY Y^e
22 1715–16
AGED 24
YEARS–3 MON-
THES &
24 DAYS.

[No. 118, 6 Row, West 4.]

HERE LYES WHAT
WAS MORTAL
OF Y^e WORTHY
NEHEMIAH JEWET,
∨ESQUIer∧
WHO DIED IANUARY
Y^e 1st 1719–20 AGED
77 · YEARS · LACKING
3 MONTHES

[No. 119, 13 Row, East 7.]

HERE LIES THE
BODY OF MR^S
PRISCILLA JEWET
ye WIFE OF MR
STEPHEN JEWET
DIED DECEMBER
ye 27th 1722 IN

yᵉ 35 YEAR OF
HER AGE HERE
BY DOTH LIE
SOLOMON OUR
WELL BELOVED
SON

[No. 120, 8 Row, East 8.]
HERE LIES Yᵉ
BODY OF MRˢ
ANNE JEWETT
WIFE OF
MR AQUILA
JEWETT DIED
MARCH Yᵉ 6ᵗʰ
1723 IN Yᵉ
40ᵗʰ YEAR OF
HER AGE

[No. 121, 8 Row, East 1.]
HERE LIES THE
BODY OF DEACON
EZEKIEL JEWETT
WHO DIED SEP
TEMBER Yᵉ 2ⁿᵈ
1723 in Yᵉ
81 YEAR
OF HIS AGE

[No. 122, 13 Row, East 8.]
HERE LIES THE
BODY OF MRˢ
SARAH JEWETT
yᵉ WIFE OF MR
STEPHEN JEWETT
WHO DIED
DECEMBER yᵉ 3ᵈ
1724 IN yᵉ
49 YEAR
OF HER AGE

[No. 123, 16 Row, West 1.]
HERE LIES Yᵉ BODY
OF MRˢ REBEKAH JEWET
yᵉ WIFE OF MR
JOSEPH JEWET WHO
DIED DECEMBER Yᵉ 26ᵗʰ
1729 IN Yᵉ 74ᵗʰ
YEAR OF HER AGE

[No. 124, 19 Row. West 1.]
HERE LIES Yᵉ BODY
OF MRˢ MARY JEWET
Yᵉ WIFE OF MR
JOSEPH JEWET WHO
DIED JUNE Yᵉ 26
1732 in Yᵉ 43
YEAR OF HER AGE

[No. 125, 12 Row, East 3.]
HERE LIES Yᵉ
BODEY OF ELISABETʰ
JEWET yᵉ DAFTᴿ OF
MR EPHRAIM JEWET
WHO DIED APREL
yᵉ 5 1737 IN yᵉ
12 YEAR OF HER
AGE

11

[No. 126, 12 Row, East 4.]
HERE LIES Y^e
BODEY OF MR
EPHRAIM JEWET
WHO DIED DECEMBER
Y^e 13   1739 IN
Y^e 59 YEAR OF HIS
AGE

[No. 127, 11 Row, East 4.]
HRE LIES Y^e
BODEY OF MR^s
ELISABETH JEWETT
THE WIFE OF MR
JACOB JEWETT
WHO DIED SEPTEMB^R
Y^e 17 1741 IN Y^e
31 YEAR OF
HER AGE

[No. 128, 12 Row, East 5.]
HERE LYES BURIED
THE BODY OF M^r
THOMAS JEWET
WHO DYED JULY
Y^e 1st 1742
IN THE 75th YEAR
OF HIS AGE

[No. 129, 18 Row, West 1].
HERE LIES Y^e
BODY OF MR^s
RUTH JEWET
Y^e WIFE OF MR
ELIPHELET JEWET
WHO DIED SEPTEM^r
18   1750
IN Y^e 37
YEAR OF HER
AGE

[No. 130, 13 Row, East 10.]
Here Lies The
Body of Mrs Lyda
Jewett The Wife of
Mr Stephen Jewett
Who Died Sept^r
the 7 1754
in ye 70 Year of
HER AGE

[No. 131, 1 Row, East 7].
To The Memory of
Mrs Elizabeth Jewett
She was a virtuous
and Amiable Consort
To the Revd Jedidiah
Jewett and Died
Suddenly April
The 14th 1764
Æta   51
Proh Dolor

[No. 132, 13 Row, East 9.]

HERE LIES BURIED
THE BODY OF
CORNET STEPHEN
JEWETT WHO
DEPARTED THIS
LIFE JANU^r THE
14^h 1771 IN
THE 88^h YEAR
OF HIS AGE

[No. 133, 26 Row, West 1.]

HERE LIES INTRR'^{d}
THE BODY OF
Mrs ELISABETH
JEWETT CONSORT
OF Mr JACOB
JEWETT JUN^r
WHO DEPARTED
THIS LIFE JULY
THE 29^h 1773
ÆTAT 26
TIME HOW SHORT
ETERNITY HOW LONG.

[No. 134, 2 Row, East 6.]

Here lies Buried
the Body of
Mr JOSEPH JEWETT
died Augst ye 1st 1774
In ye 36th Year
of his Age

[No. 135, 2 Row, East 11.]

HERE LIES BURIED
THE BODY OF
Mr JACOB
JEWETT WHO
DEPARTED THIS
LIFE MAY THE
26th A D 1774
AND IN THE
66th YEAR
OF HIS AGE

[No. 136, 2 Row, East 5.]

In Memory of

Mrs RUTH JEWETT
Dau^r of Capt GEORGE &
Mrs HANNAH JEWETT
who died Sep^t ye 29 1774
In ye 29th year of her Age

Youth consider and know that no
Age is exempt from the shafts of Death

[No. 137, 1 Row, East 6.]

In Memory of
Capt George Jewett
who died Feb^{ry} ye 5th 1776
Aged 68 years

The memory of the Just is Blest
When in the Silent Grave they rest
Free from the anxious cares and strife
Mans Portion in this mortal Life
Reader behold reflect and know
That by Deaths Darts all men must go
To Realms of happiness or Woe

[No. 138, 18 Row, West 2.]

To the Memory
of
Mr Eliphalet Jewett
who died
Oct. 30, 1789
In the 78th Year
of his Age

[No. 139, 22 Row, West 3.]

In Memory
of   MR·^{s}
Mary Jewett
who died
Augst 26th 1794
aged 60
years

[No. 140, 23 Row, West 8.]

In Memory of
Mrs Abigail Jewett,
wife of
Capt Moses Jewett,
who departed this Life
Nov 8th 1794
Aged 72 years

The rising morning can't assure
That we shall end the day ;
For death stands ready at the door
To take our lives away.

[No. 141, 22 Row, West 4.]

In Memory of
MRS MARY JEWETT
Relict of
Mr Jeremiah Jewett
who died Febr^y 17th 1796
In the 91st year of
her age

She Fear'd the Lord obey'd his voice
hop'd in his word and died of choice

[No. 142, 23 Row, West 7.]

In Memory of
CAP^T MOSES JEWETT,
who departed this Life
July 31st 1796
In the 75th year
of his age

[No. 143, 9 Row, West 6.]

Memento mori
Numerare Patribus Umbra quietis
In Memory of
Mr. David Jewett,
Companion of Mrs Elisabeth
Jewett, who died July 15th 1799
Ætat. 53.

The voice of God call'd, anon I obey'd,
Resign'd my life, & nature's debt I paid
My fabric now sleeps, my labours are o'er,
My spirits landed on the boundless shore.
Nor you friends, can death, God's messenger stay,
But must repose too, in mouldering clay,
Then your golden days improve, as they haste,
Living joys flowing from Religion taste.

Be wise, love mercy, humbly with God walk
Then vice can't proffered fruitions mock.
That you may sing, in Canaan's liberty,
O death, grave, where are thy sting & victory.

[No. 144, 1 Row, East 5.]

In memory
of
HANNAH JEWETT
Relict of
Cap.t George Jewett
who died
Sep.r 28 1799
Æt 93

My flesh shall slumber in the ground,
Till the last trumpets joyful sound
Then bust the chains with sweet surprise
And in my Savours image rise

[No. 145, 18 Row, West 5.]

Priscilla Jewett
died
Sept.r 1805
in her
69th year

[No. 146, 6 Row, West 10.]

In Memory of
William Jewett,
Son of
Joseph & Hannah Jewett,
who died Feb.y 24th 1809.
in the 21st Year
of his Age

Here in the silent grave I lie!
No more the scenes of life to try!
And you dear friends, I leave behind,
Must soon this gloomy mansion find.

[No. 147, 6 Row, West 8.]
Mr
JOSEPH JEWETT
died
July 10. 1819
Æt. 71.

"Mortals, how few among your race;
Have given this thought its weight;
That on this present moment hangs
Your everlasting Fate."

[No. 148, 9 Row, West 4.]
In memory of

MR JONATHAN JEWETT,
who died
August 26, 1824.
Aged 51.

Stop dear friends and drop your tears,
I must lay here till Christ appears.

[No. 149, 9 Row, West 5.]
In memory of
MRS ELIZABETH JEWETT
Relict of
Mr David Jewett;
who died
Dec. 8, 1824
Aged 77

Blessed are the dead, that die
in the Lord

[No. 150, 6 Row, West 9.]
Mrs
HANNAH
relict of
Mr Joseph Jewett
died Oct. 13. 1826.
Æt. 74.

O, hast thou made thy peace with God
Or art thou still in nature's road;
If so, repent, believe, obey,
Ere death shall snatch thy breath away.

[No. 151, 13 Row, West 12].
IN
Memory of
SARAH JEWETT
who died
Sept. 5th AD. 1828.
Aged 51 y^s.

[No. 152, 1 Row, East 11.]
Here Lie Intered
The mortal remains of
Mr. Paul Jewett &
Mrs. Jane Jewett his wife, &
Daughter Mary Bishop.
PAUL JEWETT
Died Aug. 29, 1828 aged 89
JANE JEWETT
Died April 29, 1811; aged 74
MARY BISHOP
Died Nov. 26, 1801; aged 38
This stone also commemorates all the
Children of Paul & Jane Jewett. Viz.
1. PAUL, who died at Lansingburg, N. Y.
     Oct. 23 1777; aged 17 y^{rs}.
2. RUTH J. HALE, died
     Oct. 17, 1839; aged 73.
3. EDNAH J. CUSHING, died at
   Providence, R. I. April 24, 1815; aged 42
4. ELIPHALET died at Boston
     April 19, 1837; aged 61.
5. Rev. PAUL died at Hamilton,
     May 15, 1840; aged 60.
          JANE J. PABODIE
     of Providence, R. I. &
JOSHUA JEWETT, who erected
     this stone still survive, in Nov. 1844

[No. 153, 11 Row, West 1.]

HERE LYES Y^e BODY OF
Mrs HANNAH JOHNSON
WIDDOW OF CAP^t JOHN
JOHNSON WHO DIED
DECEMBER Y^e 25 1717
AGED 83 YEARS

[No. 154, 13 Row, West 1.]

HERE LIES Y^e BODY
N
OF HANNAH JOHNSO
Y^e DAUGHTER OF
MR SAMUEL AND
MR^S FRANCIS JOHN
SON WHO DIED
SEPTEMBER Y^e 22ND
1723 IN THE 19th
YEAR OF HER AGE

[No. 155, 12 Row, East 2.]

HERE LIES Y^e BODYES
OF Y^e SONS OF MR DANIEL
JOHNSON FRANCIS JOHNSON
DIED AUGUST Y^e 18 1737
IN Y^e 11th YEAR OF HIS AGE
JUDAH DIED SEPTEMBER Y^e
14th 1736 IN Y^e 7th YEAR OF
HIS AGE OBADIAH DIED
JUNE Y^e 9th 1736 IN Y^e
3 YEAR OF HIS AGE
ISAIAH DIED SEPTE^M Y^e
24 1736 AGED A 11
MONTHS AND 7 DAYS

[No. 156, 13 Row, East 6.]

HERE LIES ye BODEY OF
MR^S HANNAH JONSON Y^e
WIFE OF MR DANIEL JONSON
WHO DIED FEBRUARY Y^e 19th
1740 IN Y^e 35 YEAR OF
HER AGE WITH THEAR
CHILD ELIZABETH THAT
DIED MAY Y^e 1 1740
BING 1 YEAR & 6 MONT^S
& 6 DAYS OLD

[No. 157, 11 Row, West 2.]

Here Lies Y^e Body
of Abigah Johnson y^e
Son of Mr Jonathan
& Mrs Hannah
Johnson Who Died
May the 29th
1756 in the 21
Year of his Age

[No. 158, 7 Row, West 1.]

MERIAH KILL
BORN DIED
SEP^t Y^e 23, 1710
AGED, 14 YEARS.
here Lys meriah
kiLborn in ye dust
uNteL ye resurectioN
of ye just

[No. 159, 15 Row, West 2.]

HERE LIES
Y^e BODY OF
JOSEPH
KILBURN
WHO DIED
MARCH Y^e
6 1723 IN
Y^e 40th YEAR
OF HIS
AGE

[No. 160, 16 Row, East 7.]

HERE LIES THE BODY
OF DOC^T ELIPHELET
KILBORN WHO DIED
JUNE THE 4th 1752 IN
THE 46 YEAR OF HIS AGE

NOW HE IS GONE OUR
GREAF WE CAN^T EXSPRES
AND TAKEN FROM HIS
FORMER USEFULNES

[No. 161, 24 Row, West 8.]

In Memory of
Mrs DOROTHY KILBORN,
Wife of
Mr Joseph Kilborn
who died Aug. 12th 1793,
in the 63rd year of her age
Erected by her Brother
Francis Pickard

[No. 162, 11 Row, West 3.]

HERE LYS THE BODY OF
EZEKIEL LAITEN THE
SON OF EZEKIEL AND REBE
KAH LAITEN WHO DYED

AUGUST 24 1716 IN THE
21 YEAR OF HIS AGE
AS YOU ARE SOWARE WE
AS WE ARE SO YOU WILL
BE

[No. 163, 11 Row, West 4.]

HERE LIES Y^e
BODY OF EZEKIEL
LAITON WHO
DIED NOU^E
Y^e 21th 1723
IN THE 66
YEAR OF
His AGE

[No. 164, 9 Row, East 4.]

HERE LIES Y^e BODY
OF JONATHAN
LAMBERT Y^e SON ^{OF}
MR THOMAS &
MR^s SARAH LAMBERT
WHO DIED
JANUARY Y^e 5th
172$^4/_5$ IN Y^e 7th
YEAR OF HIS AGE

[No. 165, 9 Row, East 3.]

HERE LIES Y^e
BODY OF EDNAH
LAMBERT DAFTER
OF MR THOMAS &
MR^s SARAH LAMBERT
WHO DIED MARCH Y^e
13 1729 IN Y^e 21
YEAR OF HER AGE

[No. 166, 9 Row, East 2.]

HERE LIES Y^e BODY
OF LUCI LAMBERT
DAUGHTER OF THOMAS
LAMBERT ESQ. WHO
DIED MAY Y^e
15 1736 IN
THE 15 YEAR
OF HER
AGE

[No. 167, 15 Row, East 2.]

HERE LIES Y^e
BODY OF MR^s
ELIZABETH
LAMBERT THE
WIFE OF MR THOM
AS LAMBERT WHO
DIED JULY Y^e 6
1749 AGED 36
YEARS 3 MONTHS
& 10 DAYS

[No. 168, 17 Row, East 7.]

Here Lies The
Body of Mrs
Deborah Lambert Y^e
Wife of Mr Nathan
Lambert Who died
January ye 25
1754 in the 38
Year of her Age

[No. 169, 16 Row, East 1.]

Here Lies Buried The
Body of yᵉ Honʳᵈ Thomas
Lambert Esq Who
Died June the 30 A D
1755 Aged 77
Years 2 Months
And 22 Days

[No. 170, 16 Row, East 2.]

HERE LIES BURIED
THE BODY   OF
Mʳˢ SARAH LAMBERT
RELICT OF THE HONRᴸᴸ
THOMAS LAMBERT ESQʳ
WHO DEPARTED THIS
LIFE JULY THE 11ᵗʰ
A D 1759 IN
THE 77ᵗʰ YEAR
OF HER AGE

[No. 171, 4 Row, West 8
(Marble).]

WILLIAM LAMBERT,
Born
July 22, 1772
Died
Dec. 11, 1824.

[No. 172, 15 Row, East 3.]

In Memory of Cornet
Thomas Lambert who
Deceased April the 17ʰ
1775 Æt 63
Behold Inscribed Upon
This Stone the Parent
Kind the Patient
Son the Friendly
Grones the childrens
Cries could not
Avail Lo Here
He lies

[No. 173, 16 Row, East 3.]

Memento mori
In Memory of
THOMAS LAMBERT Esqʳ.
who departed this life
Decʳ yᵉ 11ᵗʰ AD 1793
Ætat. 45

Let friends & strangers mark this stone
Reflect & feel & sigh and mourn
At Deaths alarms prepare to go
The Way the living cannot know

[No. 174, 15 Row, East 4.]

Sacred
To the Memory of
Mrs Anna Lambert,
Relict of Cornet Thos Lambert,
who departed this Life
Augst. 28th 1806. Æt 83
Also in Memory of
Alfred son of
Jon^a & Hannah Lambert,
who died Augst. 24th 1807. Aged
16 Months & 15 days.

[No. 175, 16 Row, East 4.]

Mrs
APPHIA
relict of Thomas Lambert, Esq.
died Nov. 24. 1825.
Æt. 77.

[No. 176, 4 Row, West 9 (Marble).]

Mr THOMAS LAMBERT,
Died
March 6, 1825
Aged 43.

And as we have borne the image of
the earthy, we shall also bear the
image of the heavenly

An Infant Son of
DAVID & OLIVE L. SMITH,
Died Sept. 29, 1836

[No. 177, 14 Row, West 5 (Marble Monument).]
[North front.]

JOHN LAMBERT
Died June 21, 1827
Aged 48 yrs
& 3 mos
SARAH B.
his wife
Died March 18, 1865
Aged 83 yrs
& 4 mos

A stricken family mourn their loss

LAMBERT

[West front]

NATHAN LAMBERT
Died July 18, 1831
Aged 78 yrs.
ABIGAIL P.
his wife
Died Jan. 4, 1814
Aged 61 yrs.

[East front]

HANNAH B.
Daughter of
John & Sarah B.
LAMBERT
Died Sept. 15, 1842
Aged 27 yrs
EMILY L RICHARDS,
Daughter of
John & SarahB.
LAMBERT
Died Aug. 1, 1868
Aged 56 yrs

[No. 178, 16 Row, East 8.]

Here lies The Body of
Mrs Dorothy Lancaster
the Wife of Mr Thomas
Lancaster Who Died
June the 23 1752
in the 52 year
of her Age

[No. 179, 24 Row, West 6.]

In Memory of
MR THOMAS LANCASTER,
who fell asleep Decr. 29th 1792,
in the 90th year of her age.
Also
ANNA LANCASTER
Daughter of Samuel &
Hitty Lancaster,
who died Decr. 12th 1793
aged 1 year 3 months.

The sleeping dead shall wake to sleep no more
But live all glorious by their Judges power
Are these the forms that mouldered in the dust
And the transcendent glories of the just

[No. 180, 24 Row, West 5.]

In memory of
LYDIA LANCASTER,
who died Sept. 2nd 1829,
aged 40 yr^s. and 6 mo^s.

That once lov'd form, now cold & dead,
Each mournful thought employs,
And nature weeps her comforts dead
And wither'd all her joys.

[No. 181, 11 Row, East 7.]

HERE LIES
Y^e BODY OF
JOHN MANNING
Y^e SON OF JOHN
& JANE
MANNING WHO
DIED AUGUST
Y^e 12   1736
AGED 4 YEARS

[No. 182, 15 Row, East 10.]

HERE LYES BURIED
THE BODY OF M^{rs}.
HANNAH MIGHILL
THE WIFE OF M^r.
THOMAS MIGHILL
WHO DIED SEPT^R.
Y^e 25th   1748
IN THE 21st YEAR
OF HER AGE

[No. 183, 15 Row, East 14.]

A Son
of Deaⁿ. Thomas*
& Sarah Mighill
born & Died
Augst Ye
6th 1761

[No. 184, 17 Row, East 3.]

HERE LIES BURIED
CAP^t NATHANIEL
MIGHILL WHO
DEPARTED THIS
LIFE AUGUST
THE 25^h A D
1761 AND
IN THE 78^h
YEAR OF
HIS AGE

[No. 185, 17 Row, East 2.]

Here lies the Remains
of Mr NATHAN^L MIGHILL
Son of Mr JEREMIAH &
Mrs SARAH MIGHILL
who Died Augst ye 5th
1773 Aged 14 Years
Who with his Dying breath
recomemded Jesus Christ
to a Perishing world longing
himself for the full injoyme't
of him as his only Savoiur
& everlasting Portion

[No. 186, 17 Row, East 4.]

Here lies the Remains of
Mrs PRISCILLA MIGHILL
Consort of
Capt NATHANIEL MIGHILL
Who Departed this Life
Feb^{ry} ye 26th 1776
In ye 94th Year
of her Age

[No. 187, 15 Row, East 11.]

In Memory of
Mrs SARAH MIGHILL
wife of Deacon
Thomas Mighill
Deces^d June 1st 1778
In ye 58th Year
of her Age

[No. 188, 2 Row, East 2.]

[Footstone in place of headstone broken and lost.]

Mrs Elizabeth
Mighill, at whose
feet lies buried her
grandchild Miss
Priscilla Pearly
Aged 15 months & 4 D'

[No. 189, 2 Row, East 3.]

Memento Mori

Sacred to

the Memory of

NATHANIEL MIGHILL ESQ,

who having served his country

as a Justice of the Peace and Repre-

sentative to the General Court of

this state for many years

Departed this Life March the 26th

AD 1788   Aged 73 years.

A pious Christian and a friend sincere
A husband tender, to his Children dear,
Virtue in him a friend could find,
To him twas pleasing to be kind,
He's gone alas, nor could he stay
To serve his Maker here in clay
His spirit still we hope does sing
The Praise of God his heavenly king.

[No. 190, 23 Row, West 5.]

Memento mori

In Memory of

Mr JEREMIAH MIGHILL

who departed this life

Octr ye 3^d. AD 1793

Ætat. 69

Blessed are They, and only They,
Who in the Lord the Saviour die.
Their Bodies wait Redemption's Day
And sleep in Peace where e'er they lie.

[Foot stone.]

M^r J Mighill

Nathaniel

son of Mr Thomas &

Mrs. Mary Mighill

Died Dec. 16 1793

aged 5 months

13

[No. 191, 23 Row, West 4.]

In Memory of
Miss ELISABETH MIGHILL
who died Feb. 15*th* 1796 *Ætat.* 22½.
(*Daughter of Mr. Jeremiah &*
Mrs Sarah Mighill. And intended
Consort of Rev. Humphrey C. Perley
of Methuen.)

The young the virtuous, fair & wise,
Though near pale death will close their eyes,
But O their flesh in hope doth rest,
Their souls will be forever blest.—
From me O friends in this cold urn,
Receive advice & cease to mourn,
Gird up your loins for death prepare
And you in glory shall appear.

[No. 192, 15 Row, East 12.]

In Memory of
ANNA
Daughter of Dea.
Thomas Mighill
who departed this life
June 23 1796 :
in the 13, *year*
of her age

This youthfull bloom was snatch'd
away, No longer in this world to
stay, For God did call & she must
go   And leave you in this world
below

[No. 193, 23 Row, West 6.]

Mrs Sarah Mighill
Relict of
*M*r *Jeremiah Mighill,*
died, Feb. 18th 1799,
Ætat. 63.

Thy mortal beauty, with thy body fades & dies,
Thy Christian meekness, with thy soul ascends the skies
The part well done, which God to the was pleas'd to give,
Thy faithful spirit will the shining stars out-live.

[No. 194, 15 Row, East 13.]

Sacred to the memory of
Dea THOMAS MIGHILL Esq
who died
Aug. 26th 1807
in his 86th year

Beneath this sculptur'd stone is laid,
The Saint and Patriots hoary head.
Who long was taught in virtues school
To live by faith and walk by rule

Christs Sheep and Lambs with wine and bread
In plenty from his hands were fed;
And now we trust his sweet repast
Of heavenly wine, will ever last.

Reader, your turn will come to die!
Your body in the grave must lie!
Follow the path this Saint has trod,
And you shall find your Savor God.

[No. 195, 11 Row, West 5.]

ELIZABETH MIGHILL
Daughter of Mr Thomas &
Mrs Mary Mighill
Died Aug. 8. 1816.
Æt. 20.

Let weeping virtue mourn around her tomb,
And pious friendship wail her early doom,
Yet worth like her's, sustains no rude decay,
Tho' time should sweep these sculptur'd lines away,
Here with the ills of life her sorrow ends,
The best of daughters, sisters, and of friends.

[No. 196, 11 Row, West 6.]

Mr
THOMAS MIGHILL
died
Feb. 8. 1821
Æt. 55.

Look down upon this sacred spot and see
What death can do to you as well as me.
Dear bosom friend, your falling sand is nigh,
Children prepare 'tis God that calls on high
Neighbors and friends you soon must be the same,
Prepare for death but in the savior's name.

[No. 197, 11 Row, West 7.]

Mrs.
MARY
Relict of
Mr Thomas Mighill
died Feb. 8. 1824
Æt. 55.

The pains she long endur'd are now no more,
Her body moulders in the silent tomb.
But gone we trust, to some more blissfull shore
Her spirit reigns where joys unfading bloom.

[No. 198, 15 Row, East 15.]

Mrs.
RACHEL
relict of
Dea?. *Thomas Mighill,*
died June 17, 1824
Æt. 80.

[No. 199, 11 Row, West 8
(Broken).]

MR
JEREMIAH MIGHILL,
DIED
SEPT. 8   1834
Æt. 36.

There was a time, that time is past,
When Youth! I bloomed like thee;
A time will come, 'tis coming fast,
When thou shalt fade like me.

[No. 200, 5 Row, West 1.]

HERE LYS BURIED M^r
THOMAS NELSON
WHO DIED APRIL Y^e 5
1712 AGED 77 YEARS
Who Liv'd a saintLike harmLes Life
Lov'd ᴀʟʟ ɢood books but ɴo bad striꜰe
Who dy'd a quiet easie death
& to christ resigɴ'd his breath
So Liue my soɴs my christ o seek
& when you die Like christ be meek

[No. 201, 13 Row, West 7.]

HERE LYES Y^e BODY
OF ABIGAIL NEL-
SON (DAUGHTER
OF THOMAS &
HANAH NELSON)
DIED AUGUST Y^e
18   1716   AGED
2)   YEARS.

[No. 202, 17 Row, East 1
(Marble).]

MARY SOPHIA,
Dau^r of
Stephen M. & Apphia L.
NELSON,
Born Nov. 27, 1802,
Died Dec. 9, 1805,
Aged 3 yrs. & 12 ds.

[No. 203, 10 Row, East 4.]

HERE LIES Y^e
BODY OF CAP^T
EZEKIEL NORTHEND
WHO DIED DECEMB^R
THE   23   1732
IN Y^e   66th   YEAR
OF HIS   AGE

[No. 204, 11 Row, East 3.]

HERE LIES Y^e BODYES
OF MOSES & JOHN
NORTHEND SONS OF MR
SAMUEL & MRS MARY
NORTHEND MOSES DIED
AUGUST Y^e 15 & IOHN
Y^e 22 1736 MOSES IN
HIS 5 & IOHN IN Y^e
3 YEAR OF THARE AGE

[No. 205, 14 Row, East 6.]

HERE LIES Y^e
BODY OF MR
EZEKIEL NORTHIN^D
WHO DIED OCTOB^R
Y^e 18 1742 IN
Y^e 46 YEAR OF
HIS AGE

[No. 206, 15 Row, East 1.]

HERE LIES Y^e
BODY OF SAMUEL
NORTHEND WHO
DIED JUNE Y^e 15th
1749 IN Y^e 23^d
YEAR OF HIS AGE
THE ONLY SON
OF LIEUT JOHN
& MR^S BETHIAH
NORTHEND

[No. 207, 24 Row, West 1.]

HERE LIES BURIED THE
BODY OF M^{RS}
BETHIAH THE WIFE
OF CAP^T JOHN
NORTHEND WHO
DECEASED JUNE THE
12^h 1767 IN
THE 79^h YEAR
OF HER AGE

[No. 209, 14 Row, East 5.]

Memento mori

Sacred to the Memory of
Mrs ELISABETH NORTHEND
the amiable & virtuous Relict
of Mr Ezekiel Northend,
who calmly breathed her soul
into the arms of her Saviour
on the 9th of May 1787 in
the 91st Year of her Age

[No. 208, 24 Row, West 2.]

HERE LIES BURIED THE
BODY OF CAP^T
JOHN NORTHEND
WHO DECEASED
MARCH THE 24^h
AD 1768 IN
THE 76^h YEAR
OF HIS AGE

This Mournful stone as a faithful
monument of virtue fled to Realms
above & a solemn Moniter to all
below the stars, is with profound
Respect erected by her Grandson
Northend Cogswell

[No. 210, 22 Row, West 1.]

HERE LIES Y^e BODY
OF JANE OSBORN Y^e
DAUGHTER OF MR JOHN
& MR^S JANE OSBORN
WHO DIED MAY Y^e
11th 1749 AGED 5 YEA^S
AND 8 MONTHS

[No. 211, 10 Row, East 2.]

HEAR LIES MRS
MARY PALMER THE
WIFE OF DEACON
SAMUEL PALMER
WHO DIED IUNE
Y^e 7th 1716
AGED 64 YEARS

[No. 212, 10 Row, East 1.]

HERE LYES Y^e
BODY OF DECON
SAMUEL PALMER
WHO DIED JUNE
Y^e 21 1719
AGED 75 YEARS

[No. 213, 16 Row, West 7.]

HERE LIES Y^e BODY
OF PATIENCE PALMER
Y^e WIFE OF
TIMOTHY PALMER
WHO DIED JANUARY
Y^e 20th 1730 IN
Y^e 33 YEAR OF
HER AGE

[No. 214, 8 Row, East 7.]

HERE LIES MRS
JANE PAYSON Y^e
WIFE OF MR
ELIPHALET
PAYSON DIED
NOUEMBER THE
24 1722 IN
THE 24th YEAR
OF HER AGE

[No. 215, 1st Row, East 9.]

HERE LIES Y^e
BODY OF MR^s
HANNAH PAYSON
Y^e DAUGHTER OF
Y^e REUEREND MR
EDWARD PAYSON
WHO DIED THE
5 OF DECEMBER
1725 AGED
27 YEARS

[No. 215, 11 Row. East 2.]

HERE LIES
Y^e BODY OF
MR DAUID
PAYSON WHO
DIED AUGUST
Y^e 9th 1734
AGED 29
YEARS

[No. 216, 11 Row, East 5.]

HERE LIES Y^e
BODYES OF ELIPHELET
JANE AND MARK
PAYSON CHILDREN
OF MR ELIPHELET &
MR^s EDNAH PAYSON
ELIPHELET DIED IN MAY
1736 IN Y^e 9 YEAR
OF HIS AGE JANE IN
Y^e 6 YEAROFHER
AGE MARK IN Y^e
3 YEAR OF HIS
AGE

[No. 217, 2 Row, East 10.]

HERE LIES BURIED
THE BODY OF
Mrs MARY THE
WIFE OF LEIU^T
ELIOT   PAYSON
WHO   DIED
SEP^t   THE   8
A   D   1758   IN
THE   59th   YEAR
OF HER AGE

[No. 218, 23 Row, West 2.]

HERE LIES BURIED
THE BODY OF
DEACON EDWARD
PAYSON   WHO
DECEASED MARCH
THE 1^t 1769
IN THE   75^h
YEAR   OF
HIS   AGE

[No. 220, 2 Row, East 9.]

HERE LIES BURIED
THE   BODY   OF
LIEU^t   ELIOT
PAYSON WHO
DEPARTED THIS
LIFE MAY THE
4th   AD   1774
AND   IN
THE   75^h
YEAR   OF
HIS   AGE

[No. 219, 23 Row, West 3.]

HERE LIES BURIED
THE   BODY   OF
M^{rs}   PHEBE   THE
WIFE   OF   DEACON
EDWARD PAYSON
WHO DIED NOUE^M
THE   12th   1765   IN
THE   75th   YEAR
OF HER   AGE

[No. 221, 1 Row, East 1.]

In Memory of
Mrs HANNAH PAYSON
Consort of
Capt Edward Payson
Who died Decr. 19th 1784
Ætat. 54

[No. 222, 1 Row, East 2.]

In Memory of
Capt. EDWARD PAYSON
who departed this life
October 28th 1797
Ætat 69

[No. 223, 19 Row, West 2.]

Here lies buried the earthly remains
of Mary Payson, youngest
daughter of Mr Moses Paul &
Mrs Deborah Payson.

who died Sept. 17th 1801

Ætat 19.

How short and hasty are our lives
An Inch or two of time
Man is but vanity and dust
In all his flower and prime

[No. 224, 17 Row, West 5.]

FANNY,
wife of
DAVID PAYSON.
Youngest daughter
of Daniel &
Eunice Nourse.
DIED
Dec. 9, 1808,
Aged 29.

Blessed are the dead who die in the Lord

[No. 225, 5 Row, West 3
(Marble).]

SACRED
to the memory
OF
MOSES P. PAYSON,
who died
Nov. 19, 1822;
in the 80th year
of his age.

———— | ————

DEBORAH, his wife, &
daughter of
Col. Thomas & Apphia Gage,
died Dec. 9, 1833, Aged 88.

[No. 226, 9 Row, East 6.]
HERE LIES Y^e BODY
OF CAP^T JOHN
PERSON WHO
DIED MARCH Y^e
12th 1723 IN Y^e
79th YEAR OF
HIS AGE

[No. 227, 9 Row, East 5.]
HERE LIES Y^e BODY
OF MR^s MARY PEARSON
RELICT OF CAP^T JOHN
PEARSON WHO DIED
APRIL Y^e 12th 1728
IN Y^e 77th YEAR
OF HER AGE

14

[No. 228, 12 Row, East 1.]

HERE LIES THE
BODYS OF JOHN
ᵒJOSEPH & RICʰARD PEARSONS
Yᵉ SONS OF MR JOHN
PEARSON   JOHN DIED MAY
Yᵉ 11ᵗʰ 1736 IN THE 8 YEAR
OF HIS AGE   JOSEPH DIED
APRIL Yᵉ 25 1736 IN Yᵉ
6 YEAR OF HIS AGE
RICHARD DIED APRIL Yᵉ
27 AGED 2 WEEKS &
3 DAYS

[No. 229, 16 Row, East 5.]

HERE LIES THE
BODY OF MR
JOSEPH PEARSON
WHO DIED JULY
THE 19 A D 1753
IN THE 76 YEAR
OF HIS AGE

[No. 230, 17 Row, East 6.]

Here lies the Body of
Mʳˢ ELIZABETH PEARSON
Dauʳ of Capᵗ JOHN &
Mʳˢ RUTH PEARSON, who
departed this Life May
yᵉ 7ᵗʰ A D 1762   In the
21ˢᵗ Year of her Age

[No. 231, 1 Row, West 11.]

MR JOHN PEARSON
departed this life
Octʳ 5. A. D. 1819:
aged 29 years

Modest & unassuming, his merit was best known
in the friendly circle.
He made a bequest of 500 dols. to the American
education society.

[No. 232, 5 Row, West 4.]

Miss
SOPHIA
Daughᵗ of Mr. Stephen &

Mrs Sally Pearson;
died March 11. 1825.
Æt. 22.

A sincere friend, a daughter dear
A sister kind, lies buried here.

[No. 233, 5 Row, West 5.]
Mr.
AMASA PEARSON,
son of Mr Stephen &
Mrs Sally Pearson,
died April 16, 1826.
Æt. 27.

Ye youth that oft may view this spot,
Whose health and prospects promise fair;
Reflect — Soon Death may be your lot;
O then to meet your God prepare

[No. 234, 8 Row, West 2.]
SACRED
to the memory of
Capt. Francis Perley
who died July 17th 1810 :
aged 65.

—— | ——

Belov'd in life, in death to memory dear,
Tis bleeding friendship wakes the sleeping tear;
And as devotion pays the tribute sigh,
A hovering spirit wafts it to the sky!

[No. 235, 2 Row, East 4.]
SACRED
To the Memory of
MRS HANNAH PERLEY
Consort of
CAP^t JOHN PERLEY
who died Sep 8 1812
Aged 58 years

Though weeping relatives thy loss deplore
Thy virtues all the human race adore
Snatched from her children by the hand of death
Calm and serenely she resigned her breath
On each revolving year and vernal morn
May choicest flowers her sacred urn adorn
And when revolving time her circuit ends
She shall bid welcome all her earthly friends
To realms of bliss where joys eternal reign
Devoid of care and uncontrol'd by pain

[No. 236, 8 Row, West 1 (Marble).]

SACRED
to the memory of
Mrs Hannah Perley
wife of
Capt Francis Perley,
who died Jan. 22. 1814:
aged 52.

——— | ———

When death's bereaving hand wakes friendship's tear,
And sorrow's swelling heart comes weeping here,
Dear to remembrance is the sweet belief,
Thy soul is ramsom'd from a world of grief.

[No. 237, 3 Row, East 3.]

HERE LYES Y^e BODY
OF Mrs JEAN PICKARD
WIFE OF Mr JOHN
PICKARD WHO DIED
FEBRUARY ye 20 1715/16
AGED 89 YEARS

FOR THIS DEPARTED SOUL
& ALL Y^e REST
THAT CHRIST HATH PURCHASED
THAY SHALL BE BLEST

[No. 238, 8 Row, East 5.]

HERE LIES
SARAH PICKERD
Y^e DAUGHTE^R
OF ^MR JONATHA^N
& JOANNA
PICKARD WH^o
DIED NOUEM
BER Y^e 16 172^2
IN Y^e 12 YEAR
OF HER AGE

[No. 239, 17 Row, West 2.]

HERE LIES Y^e BODY
OF MR^s ELISABETH
PICKARD WIFE OF
CAP^T SAMUEL PICKARD
WHO DIED JUNE Y^e
29th 1730 IN THE
62 YEAR OF HER AGE

[No. 240, 11 Row, East 1.]

HERE LIES THE BODY
OF LEF^T JONATHAN
PICKARD HO DIED
JANUARY Y^e 25
1735 IN THE
48 YEAR
OF HIS AGE

[No. 241, 21 Row, West 2.]

HERE LIES Y^e
BODY OF MR^s MARY
PICKARD THE WIF
OF MR JONATHAN
PICKARD WHO
DIED AUGERST
T$_{HE}$ 5 1748
IN THE 29
YEAR OF HER
AGE

[No. 242, 17 Row, West 1.]

HERE LIES THE
BODY OF CAPT
SAMUEL PICKARD
WHO DIED SEPTEMB^R
THE 2 A D 1751
IN THE 89 YEAR
OF HIS AGE

[No. 243, 17 Row, East 5.]

Here Lies Interrd
M^r JON^a PICKARD
Who Departed
this Life February
the 16th 1765
In the 48th Year
Of his AGE

[No. 244, 2 Row, West 2.]

HERE LIES BURIED
THE BODY OF
Mrs EDNAH Y^e
WIFE OF DEAC^N
FRANCIS PICKARD
WHO DECEASED
AUG^T THE 30^h
1769 IN THE
76^h YEAR OF
HER AGE

[No. 245, 2 Row, West 1.]

In Memory of
Deacon FRANCIES
PICKARD who died
Sept.ʳ 12, 1778.
Æt. 89

Maʳk the perfect man and behold
The upright for the end of
that man is peace

[No. 246, 2 Row, West 3.]

In Memory o f
Mᴿˢ MARY PICKARD
Wife of
Mʳ Jonathan Pickard
who departed this life
May 21ˢᵗ 1782 In
the 64ᵗʰ year of her age

[No. 247, 1 Row, West 3.]

In Memory of
Mʳˢ Sarah Pickard
wife of
Mʳ Joshua Pickard
Died April 28, 1783
In yᵉ 36 Year
of her age

Go — Dry your Tears—
& run the Christian race with
Chearfulnes — then rest your weary
heart — & sweetly slum'ring in this
dark embrace lesten the welcom
sound: "Arise yᵉ Dead."—

[No. 248, 6 Row, West 11.]

In
Memory of
JOSHUA PICKARD ESQ.
who died
March 10ᵗʰ 1814.
Æt. 69.

" But O, 'tis well! The will of God is done.
His course is finish'd, and his race is run :
Gone to repose, from sorrow, care and pain :
The loss is ours :   He reaps eternal gain.

[No. 249, 12 Row, West 7.]

Mr.
FRANCIS PICKARD
died March 11. 1816.
Æt. 91.

Here let remain undisturb'd his dust
Untill the resurection of the Just.

[No. 250, 6 Row, West 12.]

Here lay the remains of
Mrs SUSANNA PICKARD
widow of the late
Joshua Pickard Esq.
She died Oct. 15ᵗʰ 1821.
Aged 68 years.

" Though woes on woes have sadden'd thy last yeᵃʳˢ
" And anguish keen has caus'd a flood of tears ;
" Heaven wounds to heal, and marks the labouringᵇʳᵉᵃˢᵗ;
" Dissolves the night, and guides thee to thy rest."

[No. 251, 7 Row, West 2.]

HERE LYES Yᵉ BODY
OF Mʳ AaRON
PENGRY (SON OF
DECON MOSES ₕ
PENGRY OF IPSWIC
)WHO DIED : SEPTʳ
Yᵉ 19 ; 1714
AGED 63 YEARS

[No. 252, 7 Row, West 3.]

HERE LIES Yᵉ
BODEY OF MRˢ
ANN PINGRE WIDOW
OF MR ARON PINGRE
WHO DIED FEBRUARʸ
Yᵉ 3 1740 IN Yᵉ
80 YEAR OF HER
AGE

[No. 253, 13 Row, West 5.]

HERE LIES   Y^e
BODY OF MR
SAMUEL PLATS
WHO   DIED
MA^{R}CH Y^e 24
1726   IN   Y^e
78 YEAR OF
HIS AGE

[No. 254, 13 Row, West 4.]

HERE LIES THE
BODY OF MR^s MARY
PLATS Y^e WIFE OF
MR SAMUEL PLATS
WHO DIED   JUNE
Y^e 2^{nD} 1726 IN   Y^e
70th YEAR OF HER
AGE

[No. 255, 15 Row, West 6.]

SYLVIA PLUMER,
Daughter of Mr Bradstreet
& Mrs. Hannah Plumer,
died Aug. 6. 1815.
Aged 16 years 6 months
& 16 days.

So fades the lovely blooming flower
Frail smiling solace of an hour !
So soon our transient comforts fly,
And pleasure only blooms to die.

[No. 256, 15 Row, West 8.]

Mr.
SAMUEL PLUMER,
died April 14. 1817.
Æt. 80.

Stop, mortal man, and turn your eye,
Here read your doom ! prepare to die.

[No. 257, 10 Row, West 3.]

HERE LYES Y^e BODY
OF SAMUEL PRIME
WHO DIED MARCH
Y^e 4th 1717–18 AGED
43 YEARS

[No. 258, 8 Row, East 6.]

HERE LIES Y^e BODY OF
MR MARK PRIME
WHO DIED OCTOBER
Y^e 7th 1722   IN Y^e
42   YEAR   OF
HIS AGE

[No. 259, 24 Row, West 7 (Marble).]

Sacred to the Memory
OF
THOMAS PRIME,
who died May 8, 1793,
Aged 45 Yrs.
Also his wife
MARY NELSON,
who died Nov. 14, 1815,
Aged 58 Yrs.

Parents dear, we hope to meet you,
Freed from sin, in realms above,
Then with fond affection greet you
Midst the scenes of joy and love.
" For as in Adam all die even so in
Christ shall all be made alive."

[No. 260, 1 Row, West 4.]
Reader! this silent stone can tell,
When first a prey to death, my Father fell.
Thus Sons, their Sires from dark oblivion save,
Act a short part themselves, and find a grave.

Mr HUMPHREY H. RICHARDS,
died
May 28th 1783.
in the 28th year of his age

Erected by his Son M. R.

[No. 261, 24 Row, West 4.]
In Memory of
MRS JANE RICHARDS
Consort of
Mr Moses Richards
who died March 17th 1793
aged 40 Years.

And of her Infant
Daniel Richards

15

[No. 262, 13 Row, West 10.   (Marble).]

In Memory of
Mʳ MOSES RICHARDS.
who died Decʳ 2 1808
Aged 55 years

Why do we mourn departing friends
Or shake at deaths alarms?
'Tis but the voice that Jesus sends,
To call them to his arms.

The graves of all the saints be bless'd
And soften'd every bed :
Where should the dying members rest
But with their dying head?

[No. 263, 4 Row, West 1.]

HEAR LYS WHAT
WAS MORTAL OF
HENNERY RYLEE
WHO DIED MAY
Yᵉ 24 1710 & IN
Yᵉ 82 YEAR OF
HIS AGE

[No. 265, 14 Row, West 3.]

HEAR LIES MRS
SUSANNA SCOTT
Yᵉ WIFE OF MR
BENIAMIN SCOTᵀ
DIED AUGUST
Yᵉ 20ᵗʰ   1719
IN Yᵉ 69ᵗʰ YEAᴿ
OF HER AGE

[No. 264, 24 Row, West 3.]

Here Lies The
Body of Ezkiel
Sawyer who died
June 26ᵗʰ 1766
Aged 60 Years
Save one Day

[No. 266, 2 Row, West 14.]

Capt.
JOHN SCOTT
died
March 2. 1828
Æt. 71.

A tender husband, father dear,
A much lamented friend lies here.

[No. 267, 20 Row, West 3.]

IN
Memory of
MR. ISAAC SMITH,
Born Oct. 25,
1743;
Died March 17,
1816.

Also three of his children
Elizabeth born Dec. 12 1781
Died Aug. 7 1784
Edward born Aug 12 1784
Died Dec. 21 1795
David born Feb. 24 1776
Died Dec. 4. 1801

[No. 268, 15 Row, West 7 (Marble).]

Mrs
ELIZABETH B.
wife of
Capt Benjamin H. Smith,
Daughter of Mr. Bradstreet
& Mrs Ann Plummer,
died Aug. 26. 1828.
Æt. 24.

Liv'd to wake each tender passion,
And delightful hopes inspire,
Di'd to try our resignation,
And direct our wishes higher.

[No. 269, 20 Row, West 4.]

Mrs
ELIZABETH
Relict of
Mr Isaac Smith
died April 15. 1832
Æt. 84.

[No. 270, 1 Row, West 5.]

In
Memory of
JOSEPH STACY
who died March 7
1 8 0 9
Aged 43 Years.

[No. 271, 8 Row, East 3.]
HERE LYES Yᵉ BODY
OF MRS EDNER
DAUGHTER OF MR
EZEKIEL & MRS
EDNER NORTHEND
& LATE WIFE TO
INSIGNE ANDREW
STICKNEY DIED
FEBRUARY Yᵉ 7th
1722 AGED 73

[No. 272, 8 Row, East 4.]
HERE LIES THE
BODY OF MR ANDREW
STICKNE WHO DIED
APRIL Yᵉ 29 1727
AGED ABOUT
83 YEARS

No. 273, 8 Row, East (Granite
monument).]
[*West front.*]
"WILLIAM STICKNEY,
Born in
Frampton, England,
A. D. 1592,
was, with his wife
ELIZABETH,
of Boston, in N. E. in 1638,
of Rowley in 1639,
where he died
A. D. 1665.

[*North front.*]
Erected
By his Descendants,
Josiah Stickney
of Boston,
Mathew Adams Stickney
of Salem,
Joseph Henry Stickney
of Baltimore, MD.
1865."

[No. 274, 3 Row, West 1.]
In Memory
of
JOSIAH
Eldest son of Josiah &
Martha Stickney;
who died
Decʳ 19, 1798
Aged 17 years 5 mᵒ.

O my dear friends when this you see;
Think on God remember me;
See that you are prepared to die,
For judgement and eternity

[No. 275, 3 Row, West 2.]
Mrs
MARTHA
wife of
Mr. Josiah Stickney
died Oct. 2. 1815
Æt. 60
A tender Wife, a Mother dear,
A much lamented Friend, lies here ;
When Christ returns to call her forth,
The rising day, will show her worth.

[No. 276, 3 Row, West 3.]
In memory of
MR
JOSIAH STICKNEY
who died
Oct. 20. 1825.
Æt. 66.

[No. 277, 12 Row, West 5.]
HERE LYETH INTERRED
Yᵉ BODY OF ANNA SYLE
Yᵉ WIFE OF RICHARD SYLE
WHO DEPARTED THIS LIFE
Yᵉ 25 DAY OF IANUARY
ANNO DOM 1715
ETATIS SVÆ 58

[No. 278, 7 Row, West 4 (Marble).]
In memory of
MR JONATHAN TAYLOR
who died Jan. 7, 1825 ;
Æt. 70.
Also his Dauᵗʳ
ELIZABETH.
who died Feb. 6. 1796 ;
aged 7 years.
Death gives us more than was in Eden lost,
This King of terreous is the prince of peace

[No. 279, 20 Row, West 1.]

HERE LIES Y^e
BODY OF MR
DAUID TENNY
WHO DIED
MARCH Y^e 25. 1747
IN Y^e 19 YEAR
OF HIS AGE

[No. 280, 14 Row, West 1.]

HERE LYES Y^e BODy
OF Mrs LYDIAH TODD
WIFE OF M^r SA-
MUEL TODD WHO
DIED FEBRUARY
Y^e 7 1720 AGED
27 YEARS.

[No. 281, 7 Row, East 1.]

HERE LIES Y^e BODY
OF MR^s ELISABETH
TODD Y^e WIFE
OF MR JOHN
TODD WHO DIED
APRIL Y^e 5th
1725 IN THE
64th YEAR
OF HER AGE

[No. 282, 2 Row, East 13.]

HERE LIES ye BODY
OF MR^s PRiSCILLA
TODD Y^e WIFE OF
MR SAMUEL TODD
WHO DIED MAY
Y^e 25 1725 IN Y^e
63 YEAR OF HER
AGE

[No. 283, 15 Row, East 6.]

HERE LIES THE
BODY OF MR JAMES
TODD WHO DIED
JUNE THE 17 1734
IN Y^e 63 YEAR
OF HIS AGE

[No. 284, 15 Row, East 5.]

HERE LIES BURIED THE
BODY OF MRS MARY
THE WIFE OF M^R
IAMES TODD DIED
NOU^r 10 1749 IN THE
81^s YEAR OF HER AGE

[No. 285, 2 Row, East 8.]

Here Lies Buried
Mrs Hannah
Todd Wife of
Mr Jonathan
Todd Who died
April the 21^s
1774 in • The
67^h Year
of her Age

[No. 286, 2 Row, East 7.]

Here Lies Buried
The Body of
Mr Jonathan
Todd who
Departed This
Life March
The 29^h
1775 In
The 71 Year
of His Age

[No. 279, 20 Row, West 1.]

HERE LIES Y^e
BODY OF MR
DAUID TENNY
WHO DIED
MARCH Y^e 25. 1747
IN Y^e 19 YEAR
OF HIS AGE

[No. 280, 14 Row, West 1.]

HERE LYES Y^e BODy
OF Mrs LYDIAH TODD
WIFE OF M^r SA-
MUEL TODD WHO
DIED FEBRUARY
Y^e 7 1720 AGED
27 YEARS.

[No. 281, 7 Row, East 1.]

HERE LIES Y^e BODY
OF MR^s ELISABETH
TODD Y^e WIFE
OF MR JOHN
TODD WHO DIED
APRIL Y^e 5th
1725 IN THE
64th YEAR
OF HER AGE

[No. 282, 2 Row, East 13.]

HERE LIES ye BODY
OF MR^s PRiSCILLA
TODD Y^e WIFE OF
MR SAMUEL TODD
WHO DIED MAY
Y^e 25 1725 IN Y^e
63 YEAR OF HER
AGE

[No. 283, 15 Row, East 6.]

HERE LIES THE
BODY OF MR JAMES
TODD WHO DIED
JUNE THE 17 1734
IN Y^e 63 YEAR
OF HIS AGE

[No. 284, 15 Row, East 5.]

HERE LIES BURIED THE
BODY OF MRS MARY
THE WIFE OF M^R
IAMES TODD DIED
NOU^r 10 1749 IN THE
81^s YEAR OF HER AGE

[No. 285, 2 Row, East 8.]

Here Lies Buried
Mrs Hannah
Todd Wife of
Mr Jonathan
Todd Who died
April the 21^s
1774 in • The
67^h Year
of her Age

[No. 286, 2 Row, East 7.]

Here Lies Buried
The Body of
Mr Jonathan
Todd who
Departed This
Life March
The 29^h
1775 In
The 71 Year
of His Age

[No. 287, 1 Row, East 3.]

In Memory of
Mrs ELIZABETH TODD
wife of M^r ASA TODD & Second
Dau^r of Coll^o THOMAS GAGE Esqr
who died July   23^d   1776
In ye 34 Year of her Age

She was an amiable & exemplary Christian
Behaved with Patience & Meekness under
Severe bodily Pains & is now gone, we
Trust, where all Tears are
Wiped away from her Eyes

The sweet Remembrauce of the Just
Shall flourish when she sleeps in Dust

[No. 288, 4 Row, West 4.]

In memory of
GEORGE TODD Esq.
who departed this life
Aug. 18, 1801 ; in the 47
year of his   age

Mild, modest, candid, faithful to his trust,
A friend, a tender father, sleeps in dust.
Yet shall his name, like precious ointment, cheer ;
And still his early death shall call a tear.

[No. 289, 20 Row, West 5.]

In memory
of

Jonathan Todd	LUCY
who died	daughter of Jona
Decr 3, 1801	& Sally Todd
in the 50 year	who died Decr 1. 1801.
of	in the 13 year of
His age	Her age

[No. 290, 15 Row, West 5.]

In memory
of
Lieut JAMES TODD
who died
June 17th 1808
Æt. 76

Dangers stand thick through all the ground
To push us to the tomb ;
And fierce diseases wait around,
To hurry mortals home.

[No. 291, 4 Row, West 5.]

Mrs
EDNAH TODD
wife of
Mr William Todd
died Jan. 31. 1810·
Æt. 79

[No. 292, 4 Row, West 7.]

In
Memory of
Miss Elizabeth Todd
who died
August 18, 1813
aged 39

[No. 293, 4 Row, West 6.]

Mr
WILLIAM TODD
died Dec. 8. 1815.
Æt. 86.

[No. 294, 2 Row, West 9.]

Mrs
APPHIA TODD
wife of
Mr Ezekiel Todd,
died Nov. 14. 1818
Æt. 31

[No. 295, 19 Row, West 3.]

In memory of

SALLY
wife of
Jonathan Todd
died
June 12, 1838 ;
Aged 84

JEREMIAH
son of Jonathan
& Sally Todd
died
Nov. 27, 1818
Aged 27

[No. 296, 21 Row, West 4.]

In Memory of SOPHIA
Daught. of
Doct. Joseph & Mrs Polly Torrey,
who died Aug. 15th
1797
Aged $2\frac{1}{2}$ years

Sleep on my babe, & take thy rest,
God call'd thee home, he tho't it best.

[No. 297, 7 Row, East 3 (Marble).]

IN MEMORY OF
JOHN TRUMBLE,
ONE OF THE EARLY SETTLERS
OF ROWLEY:
HE WAS A TEACHER
AND TOWN CLERK.
HE DIED
JULY 17, 1657.
AND HIS WIFE
ELLEN,
WHO DIED 1648-9

ERECTED IN 1881 BY
REV. DR. DAVID TRUMBULL

[No. 298, 13 Row, West 11.]

In memory of
MEHITABLE
wife of
James Webster
who died Sep, 16, 1815
Æt. 32

She rests in hope of a future life

16

[No. 299, 10 Row, West 7.]

Mrs
ANNA
wife of
Mr John White
died Feb. 4, 1821
Æt. 73
Blessed are the dead, which
die in the LORD.

[Nc. 301, 4 Row, East 1.]

SARAH THE WIFE
OF DANIEL WICOM
DIED APRIL ye 9th
1705 & IN Ye
33d YEAR OF HAR
AGE
A tender Mother
A prudent wife
At Gods command
resind her life

[No. 303, 6 Row, West 13.]

WILLIAM WILLIAMS.
DIED
May 7, 1868,
Aged 69 y'rs.

——:——

ABIGAIL N. HIS WIFE
Died Dec. 5, 1866,
Aged 73 y'rs.

——:——

Their Children.
EUNICE F. DIED
Jan. 23, 1859, Æ. 24 y's.

—— | ——

JULIA H. DIED
Nov. 13. 1856, Æ. 20 y'rs

[No. 300, 4 Row, East 2.]

HERE LYETH BURIED
ye BODY OF CapT
DANIEL WICOM
AGED 65 YEARS
DECD APRIL ye 15
1700

[No. 302, 4 Row, East 3.]

HERE LIES
THE BODY OF
MRS LIDIEA
WICOM THE
WIFE OF CAPT
DANIEL WICOM
WHO DIED Ye
24 OF NOUEM
BER 1722
AGED 80 YEARS

[No. 304, 11 Row, East 6.]

HERE LIES Ye
BODY OF MOSES
WOOD Ye SON OF JACOB
& HANNAH WOOD
WHO DIED AUGUST
ye 8 1736 AGED
9 YEARS

[No. 305, 10 Row, East 6.]

HERE LIES Ye
BODY OF JEREMIAH
WOOD SON OF JACOB
AND HANNAH
WOOD WHO DIED
JULY ye 17 1737
AGED 11 YEARS

[No. 306, 10 Row, East 5.]

HERE   LIES
HAN^{N}AH
WOODBERY
WHO DIED
SEPTEMBER Y^e
27 · 1722 IN
THE 38 YEAR
OFF HER AGE

[No. 307, 14 Row, East 4.]

HERE LIES Y^e
BODEY   OF
HANNAH WOODMA^N
THE DAUGHTER
OF MR STEPHEN
& M^{RS} HANNAH
WOODMAN WHO
DIED FEBRUARY
ye 27   1741^{-2}
IN ye 14 YEAR
OF HER AGE

[No. 308, 20 Row, West 2.]

HERE LIES THE
BODY OF MR
JOSHUA WOODMAN
WHO DIED OCTOBER
ye 18th 1745 AGED
36 YEARS ONE
MONTH AND 14
DAYS

[No. 309, 4 Row, West 3.]

M^{r}S
DOROTHY
WOODMAN

(This is a foot stone in the place of headstone broken and lost.)

COPY OF MONUMENTS LATELY SUBSTITUTED FOR STONES REMOVED.

[No. 310, 4 Row, East (Marble)].
[West Front.]

REV. EZEKIEL ROGERS,
first minister of Rowley,
Born at Wethersfield, Essex Co.
England, A. D. 1590, a minister
in Rowley Yorkshire 17 years.
Came to this place with his
Church and flock in April
1639, died June 23, 1660.

This ancient pilgrim nobly bore
The ark of God, to this lone shore;
And here, before the throne of Heaven
The hand was raised, the pledge was given,
One monarch to obey, one creed to own,
That monarch, God; that creed, His word alone.

[Mr. Rogers died January 23, 1660-1, and was buried January 26, 1660-1.]

Here also rest
the remains of his wives.

With him one came with girded heart,
Through good and ill to claim her part;
In life, in death, with him to seal
Her kindred love, her kindred zeal.

[South front.]

REV. SAMUEL SHEPARD,
third minister of Rowley,
Born Oct. 1641,
settled colleague with
REV. MR. PHILLIPS,
Nov. 15, 1665,
died April 7, 1668.
DOROTHY FLINT, his wife,
died Feb. 12, 1668.
REV EDWARD PAYSON fourth
minister, born June 20,
1657, ordained Oct. 25, 1682,
died Aug. 22, 1732.

Also his wives
ELISABETH PHILLIPS,
and ELISABETH APPLETON.

[East front.]

REV. JEDEDIAH JEWETT,
fifth minister of Rowley,
Born 1705,
ordained Nov. 19, 1729,
died May 8, 1774.

Also his wives
ELISABETH DUMMER
and ELISABETH PARSONS.
REV. EBENEZER BRADFORD,
sixth minister born 1746,
Installed Aug. 4, 1782,
died Jan. 3, 1801.
ELIZABETH GREEN, his wife
died July 14, 1825.

[North front.]

Here rest the great and good
here they repose
after their generous toil.
A sacred band,
they take their sleep together.

Twine gratitude, a wreath for them
More deathless than the diadem.
Who, to life's noblest end,
Gave up life's noblest powers,
And bade the legacy descend
Down, down to us and ours.

Erected by the Ladies Benevolent Circle,
of the Congregational Society, Rowley,
1851.

[No. 311, 4 Row, East (Marble)].

[North front.]

Beneath this stone
are buried the remains of
SAMUEL PHILLIPS,
the second pastor
of the Church in Rowley,
He was born in Boxford, England, A. D. 1625,
Came to America, with his father,
GEORGE PHILLIPS, first minister of
Watertown, Mass., in 1630 ; was graduated
at Harvard College, in 1650, and was
settled in the Christian ministry,
in this place, in June, 1651, where he
served God and his generation faithfully
for 45 years, and died April 22, 1696.

Near this spot are buried
the remains of his wife, SARAH,
daughter of SAMUEL APPLETON, of Ipswich ;
she died 15, July, 1714 aged 86 years.

From them have descended, among others,
George Phillips, minister of
Brook Haven, L. I., New York; who died 1739,
aged 75 years.
Samuel Phillips, minister at Andover, Mass.
died June 5, 1771, aged 81 years.
Samuel Phillips, one of the founders of
Phillips Academy, Andover, died August 21, 1790,
aged 76 years.
John Phillips, founder of Phillips Academy,
Exeter, N. H., died April, 1795, aged 76 years.

[West front.]

Samuel Phillips, Lt. Gov. of Mass.
died in Andover, Feb. 10, 1802, aged 50 years.
William Phillips, a distinguished
merchant and patriotic citizen,
died in Boston, Jan., 1804, aged 82 years.
William Phillips, Lt. Gov. of Mass.
died in Boston, May 26, 1827, aged 77 years, and
John Phillips, Prest. of the Senate of Mass.
and first Mayor of Boston, died in Boston,
May 29, 1823, aged 52 years.

This monument is erected
by Jonathan Phillips, of Boston,
a descendant in the sixth generation.
A. D. 1839.

Cemetery Record Index

All names in the cemetery records have
been indexed here. Women are listed by
both maiden and married names where given.
The spelling given in the text has been
retained in the index. Thus, readers are
advised to spend some time browsing
through the index in search of peculiar
name variations.

www.ingramcontent.com/pod-product-compliance
Lightning Source LLC
LaVergne TN
LVHW051708080426
835511LV00017B/2787